A Sea of Wisdom

Ingrid Walter
Sabina Theobalds

Walter & Company
Toronto, Ontario
Canada

Originally published in 2004 by
Walter & Company of Canada in Toronto Canada.

2nd Edition

A Sea of Wisdom

ISBN 0-9736324-1-0

1. Title

Cover Design: Lisa Watts
Front Cover Artist: Stephen Murphy

Printed and bound in Canada

Contents

Acknowledgements

We would like to thank the following individuals for their assistance in the development of our book:

Austin Clarke, Madeline Blackman, David Bowen, Phyllis Bradley, Karina Guerra, Pamela Holmes, Alfredo Luaces, Boris Masip, Elaine Murphy, Stephen Murphy, Mearle Pat Phillip, Roslyn Phillip, Avril Phillips, Mildred Theobalds and Evan Williams.

I would especially like to thank David White, Bimmer, Jim and Rita White, Hope Markes, Lorraine Paepcke, Audrey Burgess, my grandmother Sybil Laughton, my mother Joan Young, my sister Tina Walter, my father Stanley Walter and Aunt Annette Lewis for their guidance and support.

Introduction

Whenever I return to Jamaica, I often want to immediately abandon my luggage and head to the sea. It seems to call out to me, as if waiting to embrace me; to soothe my body and soul with its rhythmic ebbs and flows.

I have often thought the Caribbean Sea is like an old man that has no voice but carries many tales and lessons. Those of us who have studied the history of the Caribbean, know well that the different peoples who found their way by sea to its shores have shaped much of its history. Whether they were indigenous Arawaks and Caribs or European colonizers from England, France, Spain and Holland, Africans brought to the islands as slaves or East Indians and Chinese who came as indentured servants, they all deposited their unique cultures, languages, and particular wisdom on these islands.

Over hundreds of years of intermingling, these island peoples have created an extraordinary linguistic stew, rich with common sense, and full of observation and experience. *A Sea of Wisdom, Island Proverbs,* is a book that shares with you a collection of proverbs, that open a window to the remarkable gift people from the Caribbean have, to create proverbial phrases that warn, encourage and trigger reflection. They are universal truisms with peculiar, often funny island references that are entertaining and valuable.

Given that the majority of the islands' citizens are descendants of Africans, many Caribbean proverbs are heavily influenced by oral traditions of the Ashanti, Congo and Yoruba ethnic peoples of West Africa. The majority of these island people speak a dialect, as well as the official European languages brought to the islands by the early colonizers. These dialects are infused with African, Spanish,

Dutch, French and English words, many of which are evident in whole or in part in the proverbs presented in this book.

As you read through these proverbs from Jamaica, the Bahamas, Cuba, Barbados, Antigua, St. Lucia, and the Turks and Caicos Islands, you will be intrigued by the magical use of simple elements like food, animals, insects, even plants to provide profound comments on human nature, morality, parenting, friendship, greed, and more.

In many ways, *A Sea of Wisdom* surrounds the people of the Caribbean.

Jamaica

Throughout its history, Jamaica has attracted much international attention. In colonial times, considered the jewel in England's crown, Jamaica brought the British monarchy great wealth from the production and export of high-grade sugar and intoxicating dark and white rums. It is also the country where a feisty African woman named Nanny led a guerilla army of escaped slaves, known as Maroons, into the rugged limestone terrain of the cockpit country, thwarting all efforts by British troops to re-capture them.

Approximately 500 miles south of Miami Florida, Jamaica is where internationally renowned lyricist and reggae music icon Bob Marley was born and raised. Since his death in 1981, his gravesite and home have become historic sites, attracting thousands of local and international visitors each year. Many also flock to the annual Reggae, Jazz and Calypso festivals that have become a part of the islands vibrant entertainment scene.

Jamaica is blessed with mountains, winding rivers, cascading waterfalls, tantalizing cliffs, miles of white sand beaches and crystal blue waters. It boasts numerous varieties of plant life and tropical birds and is considered a wonderland for nature lovers. Whether you are rafting on the Rio Grande, diving into the deep waters of the Blue Lagoon, climbing up the majestic Dunns River Falls or diving off Negril's infamous cliffs into the turquoise waters below, Jamaica is a breathtakingly beautiful island, rich with history.

Its people are predominantly of African descent but many are also a mix of English, Chinese and East Indian extract. Although English is the official language of the island, the majority of the people speak Jamaican "patois," a dialect that blends English and Spanish with African words and phrases.

Jamaica's remarkable cultural history coupled with the determination of its people to survive and thrive has created a rich reservoir of thought-provoking and sage proverbs. Most of the sayings continue to stand the test of time despite having origins that reach as far back as the16th century. They are used daily by islanders and can be found in Jamaica's music and in a number of the songs of the late Bob Marley. They are a treat for any adventurous mind.

Jamaican Proverbs

Human Relations

Good fren betta dan packet money.
A good friend is better than pocket money.
Friendship is more valuable than pocket money.

Lamp cawn bun widout wick.
A lamp can't burn without a wick.
Men and women need each other.

Bush 'av' yeye, stump wear hat.
Bush have eyes and a stump wears a hat.
You never know who may be watching or listening, so be discreet.

Yu cawn sidung 'pon cow back an cuss cow kin.
You can't sit down on a cow's back while cursing a cow's relative.
It is unwise to be at odds with family members especially those who you depend upon.

Fowl 'gree fe 'atch duck hegg, but im no gree fe teach duck pickney fe swim.
A chicken agrees to hatch the duck's egg but not to teach the ducklings to swim.
Do not impose on another person's generosity.

Ole fiah 'tick eezy fi ketch.
An old fire stick is easy to rekindle.
It is easy for old lovers to reunite.

Consequences

Wen snake bite yu, yu si lizard yu run.
When a snake bites you and you see a lizard you run.
When you have been harmed, you are frightened by any situation that appears similar.

'Im bruk a 'tick fe cut 'im own backside.
He broke a stick to whip his own backside.
He engineered his own downfall.

Candle no bun' tap an ' bottom.
A candle doesn't burn at both ends.
If you over exert yourself, you will burn out.

I 'ard fi keep out de deble, but it wuss fe dribe 'im out.
It is hard to keep out the devil but it is even more difficult trying to drive him out.
It is hard to stay out of trouble, but it is even harder to get out of it.

Hour may bruk wha age cawn men.
An hour may break what an age can't mend.
It takes only a short time to do irreparable harm.

A no de same day leaf drap inna wata i' rotten.
A leaf doesn't rot the same day it's dropped into water.
Don't be hasty, be patient. Some things take time to resolve.

If yu cawn tan blow no play wid tick.
If you can't stand blows don't play with sticks.
If you can't stand stress don't put yourself in stressful situations.

Wha' sweet nanny goat a go run 'im belly.
What is sweet to a nanny goat will run his belly.
Indulgence in certain pleasures can eventually cause trouble.

Li' pepper bun big man mout'.
A little pepper can burn even a big man's mouth.
A seemingly minor indiscretion can result in a major disaster.

If yu spit in di air it we fall 'pon yu.
If you spit in the air, it will fall on you.
You reap what you sow.

Evryday de bucket go a well, wan day de bottom a go drap out.
If every day you take the bucket to the well, one day the bottom will drop out.
Constant use will inevitably result in wear and tear.

Work

No every man breakfast ready de same time.
Not everyone's breakfast is ready at the same time.
Each person's fortunes are realized at different times.

Plan you plan an' wok yu plan.
Plan your plan and work your plan.
Before embarking on a project create a plan and then execute it well.

Human Nature

Yu no si fowl batty till breeze-blow come.
You won't see a fowl's bottom until a heavy breeze.
Crisis reveals a person's true nature.

Wen bull foot bruk, im nyam wid monkey.
When a bull's foot is broken, he eats with monkeys.
When the powerful fall, they often are forced to join those they once shunned.

Commanda coco an white yam no bear together.
Comando cocoa (edoe) and white yam does not bear well together.
Greedy partners can't prosper together.

Every cave ole 'av' 'im own duppy.
Every cave has it's own ghost.
Everyone and every family have their dark secrets.

Every jackass tink 'im pickney a race 'orse.
Every jack ass thinks his child is a race horse.
Every parent thinks his child is a genius.

Duppy know who fi frighten.
A ghost knows who it can frighten.
People prey on those who are vulnerable.

Trow 'tone a pen, any pig weh squeal loudest, a 'im get lik.
Throw a stone into a pen and the pig that squeals the loudest is the one who gets hit.
Throw out bait in a group and the person who protests the most is the one who has something to hide.

Si me an' live wid me a two different ting.
Seeing me and living with me are two different things.
Only close interpersonal interaction with people will reveal their true personalities.

Some people know yu a moonshine, but dark nite dem shake fiah 'tick at yu.
Some people will know you when the moon is shining but in the dark night they will shake a lighted stick at you.
Some people will only know you when you have plenty and pretend they don't know you when times are hard.

Making Choices

Hat needle bun tread.
A hot needle burns thread.
Rushing into things can be dangerous.

Barkin' save bitin'.
Barking saves you from biting.
Prevention is better than cure.

Dry bread 'pon yu table beta dan butta bread
'pon yu neighbor.
Dry bread on your table is better than
buttered bread on your neighbours'.
It is a bad idea to covet other people's possessions.
Appreciate what you have.

If yu wan haaf a bread, beg smady buy i',
but if yu wan' whole wan, buy I' yuself.
If you want half of bread, ask someone to buy it,
but if you want whole bread buy it yourself.
If you are seeking perfection, do the job yourself.

If plaantn ben know sey im nek gwine
bruk im nebber woulda shoot.
If plantain had known that its neck would break,
it never would have borne fruit.
If people know how dearly they would pay for getting
involved in certain situations they would avoid them.

Good conscience beta dan big wage.
A good conscience is better than big wages.
Honesty is the best policy.

Mawga plaantn beta dan none at all.
A thin plantain is better than none at all.
Be grateful for small mercies and make the best of what you have.

Bud caan fly 'pon one wing.
A bird cannot fly on one wing.
It is wise to strike a balance in all things.

Yu cawn stap bud fram fly ovah yu 'ead but yu can stap 'im fram making nes in deh.
You can't stop a bird from flying over your head, but you can stop it from making a nest there.
You can't prevent yourself from encountering undesirable people but you can limit your involvement with them.

Fry di big fish fus, di likkle wan afta.
Fry the big fish first and the little one after.
Attend to more important matters first and the less important ones after.

Yu no wear boot fe ketch 'ouse fowl.
You don't wear boots to catch a house fowl.
Act covertly to ensnare the enemy.

Lizard nebber know whey 'im deh, til 'im fine imself inna puss mout'.
A lizard never knows where he is until he finds himself in a cat's mouth.
Some people don't realize they are in danger until it is too late.

Believe half wah yu si and nottn dat yu hear.
Believe half of what you see and nothing of what you hear.
Be careful of drawing hasty conclusions from what you see. Also, it is often unwise to give credibility to what you hear.

Man hate yu, 'im gi yu cutacoo fe caa water,
yu smaat yu put planntn leaf in deh.
Man hates you, he gives you a basket to carry water, but if you are smart you will put a plantain leaf in it.
When people hate you, they will try to make your life difficult by giving you an impossible task, but if you are smart, you will find a way to overcome the obstacles.

If yu no wan leaf drop pon yu, tan fram under de tree.
If you don't want leaves to drop on you, don't stand under the tree.
It is wise to stay away from situations that could cause you harm.

Power

Full bag nebber ben'.
A full bag never bends.
The wealthy will never be subservient as there is no need for them to be.

Rain a fall but di dutty tough. Me belly full but me 'ungry.
Rain falls but the ground is hard. My belly is full but I am hungry.
In this land of plenty there is a lack of compassion.

Cotton tree ever so big, li axe cut 'im dung.
The cotton tree is very big and yet a little axe will cut it down.
Even the mighty can be felled by the small and insignificant.

Tree look ever so sound,
woodpecker know wha' fe do wid 'im.
The tree appears indestructible, but the woodpecker knows its weak points.
A big bully may appear indestructible,
but one who knows his/her weaknesses can subdue him/her.

Fish a deep wata no know 'ow fish a riverside feel.
A deep water fish doesn't know how a fish by the river's edge feels.
People of means are often ignorant of the suffering of the poor.

De longer de awse tail, de easier 'im can brush weh fly.
The longer the horse's tail, the easier it is for him to brush away flies.
It is much easier for the rich and powerful to overcome difficulties.

No matter how high jankrow fly, 'im av fe come a grung fe nyam.
No matter how high the John Crow (vulture) flies he has to come to the ground for food.
No matter how wealthy one is, one has to be humble at times to hold on to one's wealth.

De higher monkey clime, de moe 'im expose.
The higher the monkey climbs, the more he is exposed.
The higher one climbs up the social ladder, the more one is subject to scrutiny.

No kya how cockroach drunk, 'im nebber kraas fowl yard.
No matter how drunk the cockroach becomes he never crosses the fowl's backyard.
It is foolhardy to court danger.

Hope

Dere is a ben in every riva.
There is a bend in every river.
Every cloud has a silver lining.

Daylight show tru likkle key ole.
Daylight shows through a little keyhole.
Genuine behaviour and goodness cannot be obscured but will be revealed despite efforts to conceal it.

Dutty wata wi' put out fiah.
Dirty water will put out a fire.
Everyone can be useful.

Wan wan coco full basket.
Putting one coco in at a time will fill the basket.
Wealth can be accumulated by saving conscientiously a little at a time.

Dry stump a cane-piece no fe laugh wen cane piece ketch fiah.
A dry stump in the cane field should not laugh when the cane field catches fire.
The one that laughs at another's trouble is likely to encounter suffering also.

No call man ded till yu bury 'im.
Don't call a man dead until he is buried.
Don't be too quick to write off someone who is wounded or in dire straights.

St. Lucia

This lush, hilly, island of hot springs, sandy beaches, jazz festivals, carnivals and French influenced cuisine, was once a thorn in the side of the French and British Empires. It's warlike Carib peoples fiercely resisted attempts by the Europeans to colonize them for some 50 years. However, even after driving out the Caribs, France and England continued to battle over this tiny island. In fact, between the signing of the peace treaty with the French in 1660 and the British take-over of the island in 1814, St. Lucia changed ownership 14 times. The British held firmly onto this picturesque Caribbean island, until St. Lucia gained independence in 1979.

St. Lucia, which is today an English speaking country, boasts two Nobel laureates, Sir Arthur Lewis, who received the Nobel Prize in Economics in 1979 and the prolific poet and playwright Derek Walcott, recipient of the 1992 Nobel Prize in Literature.

Although there are many St. Lucians who are of English ancestry, the majority of the island's people are descended from African slaves who worked on the island's sugar plantations. Many are also descendants of the French aristocracy that inhabited the island during the 17th and 18th centuries.

While the Catholic religion dominates, mysterious traditions of magic and spiritualism have survived. The annual St. Lucian carnival with its colourful costumes and steel pan music are a clear reminder of the fusion of Christianity and ancient African beliefs. The "moko jumbie," a towering, wildly costumed figure on stilts, remains a prominent figure in St. Lucian folklore and a symbol of the spirit world.

The continental forces that shaped the country for centuries also heavily influenced the language of St. Lucians.

Although the colonial masters suppressed the use of African languages by their slaves, their need to communicate with them facilitated the development of Kweyol, (Creole), a patois that intertwines French with African dialects.

St. Lucia is particularly fascinating, in that despite being an English-speaking island since the 19th century, St. Lucia's Kweyol is predominantly French. This interesting phenomenon, which is explained by the island's history, has provided fascinating study for linguists.

St. Lucian proverbs represent a clear embracing of Kweyol expression by islanders. Kweyol is spoken widely throughout the country, even on radio and in parliament. The language is also now being written and there is already a Kweyol translation of the bible.

St Lucia is unique in many ways and so are its proverbs.

St. Lucian Proverbs

Human Relations

Sa ou pa konnèt pli gran pasé-ou.
What you don't know is bigger than you.
You will never know it all, so be humble.

Kanawi ka di chodyè bonda y nwè.
The pot calling the kettle black.
You shouldn't judge others.

Sè pa mwen ki kay di lanmè i sale.
It is not for me to say his hands are dirty.
Sometimes things are better left unsaid.

Koté pak-la ba, bèf ka janbé.
Where the fence is low the cow will jump.
Where there is not much love, there is often infidelity.

Zafé kabrit pa zafé mouton.
The goat's business is not the sheep's business.
Not everyone shares your concerns.

Consequences

Mizè fè makak manjé piman.
Misery causes the monkey to eat peppers.
Misery and poverty can cause people to act completely out of character.

Aché pli pèd pli.
Buy more lose more.
The more we have the more we risk losing.

Woch-la ou voyé douvan sé li ou ke swiv.
The stone that you threw in front of you is the one you will follow.
Make sure you can live with the consequences of your actions.

Lafimé pa ke soti san difé.
Smoke does not come out without fire.
If there are signs of wrongdoing or intrigue, it is likely that some misconduct or plot has happened or is about to unfold.

Pawòl an bouch pa chaj.
Word of mouth is not cheap.
Hearsay as opposed to fact can cost you dearly.

Van vanté, lavi chalviré.
The wind blows, life is turned upside-down.
Life is fragile and even minor events can cause great upheaval.

Bal fini, vyolon an sak.
The ball is ended; the violin is in the case.
You cannot change what has passed.

Human Nature

Pli ou hangnon, pli chyen deéchiwé-w.
The more you are in rags the more dogs will tear you.
The poorer you are the more likely it is that others will take advantage of you.

Sa ki ni kako an solèy ka gadé pou lapli.
Those who have cocoa out in the sun look out for the rain.
Those who have much, spend lots of time worrying about keeping their possessions.

Woch ki atè ka mandé an dlo, woch ki an dlo ka mandé atè.
Stones on land want to be in the water and stones in the water want to be on land.
People always want what others have.

Dé mal krab pa sa wèsté dan menm tou.
Two male crabs cannot live in the same hole.
Two strong willed people cannot live together.

Chyen pa'a fè chat.
A dog does not make a cat.
Not everyone has the same talents or abilities.

Solèy kouché, solsouwi déyo.
The sun sets, and the bats are out.
"When the cats are away, the mice will play."
People often get into mischief when they think no one is watching

I fé lahont sèvi kolé.
Anger covers shame.
Anger often disguises hurt.

Making Choices

Yon batiman ki koulé pa ka anpéché you lot navidjé.
A sinking ship does not prevent another from sailing.
It is wise to focus on the positive.

Pa vann lapo tig avan ou mété-y atè.
Do not sell the tiger's skin before you take it to the ground.
Don't count your chickens before they hatch.
Never spend money that is expected but not yet in your hand.

Lè janmon jwenn bon tè i ka kouri.
When the pumpkin finds good soil, it spreads out.
It is smart to capitalize on opportunities.

Ou sav sa ou kite ou pa sav sa ou ke jwenn.
You know what you left but you don't know what you will find.
Be careful, because what you leave behind may be better than what you encounter in the future.

Lè bab kamawad ou pwi difé, wouzé sa-ou.
When your friend's beard is on fire, you must douse yours.
Don't think that you are infallible. Always protect yourself.

Maléré pa péché.
Misery is not a sin.
Don't assume that all poor are bad or worthless.

Zandoli sav kilès pyébwa i ka monté.
The lizard knows which tree to climb.
The wise know where to find opportunity and how to keep out of harms way.

Chak pen ni fomaj-yo.
Each bread has its own cheese.
Each person has his or her preference.

Tété pa ka anbawasé lèstomak.
The head does not embarrass the stomach.
Let your head rule your stomach.

Sé pou-ou domi an poulayé poul pou ou sav si poul ke wonflé.
You must sleep in the chicken coop to know if the chickens are snoring.
To really know what's going on, you should rely on personal observation.

Soti an pwèlon tonbé an difé.
Out of the pot fall into the fire.
Be careful not to leave one bad situation for another.

Bat fè-la pannan I cho.
Beat the iron while it is hot.
Take advantage of opportunity when it arrives.

Twop bijou gad-manjé vid.
Too many jewels empty cupboard.
It is dumb to court bankruptcy while trying to impress others.

Ikonomizé an piti choz èk dépansé an gwan.
Economize on small things spend on big ones.
Keep the big picture in perspective.

Power

Pli poch ou plen, pli fanm enmen'w.
The more their pockets are full the more women like it.
The rich man often gets his pick of women.

Hope

Sa ki ni koumansman ni finisman.
Everything that has a beginning has an end.
Even the worst things eventually come to an end.

Vyé kannari fè bin bouyon.
An old pot makes a good stew.
It takes time to gain wisdom.

Bowik kouyon, mé li sa poté chayli byen.
The donkey is stupid, but he can carry his load well.
Everyone has talents and value.

Tout bagay sé pou on tan.
Everything is for a time.
Nothing lasts forever.

Touléjou pa nwèl.
Everyday is not Christmas.
There will always be good and bad days.

Voumyé wanyon pasé touni.
It's better to be in rags than to be naked.
It is better to have something than nothing at all.

The Bahamas

The Islands of the Bahamas cover some 100,000 square miles, which include the southwest Atlantic Ocean, the tip of Florida and the edge of the Caribbean Sea near Haiti. Its waters are warm and clear offering visitors and local Bahamians access to 700 islands and islets covered with greenery, exotic blossoms and sandy beaches. Some like Abaco, Andros, Cat Island, Eleuthera, Grand Bahamas and Long Island are quite large. However many who visit the Bahamas, often sneak off by boat on romantic getaways, claiming small-uninhabited islands to themselves, as they sun on pristine beaches and bathe in inviting waters.

The Bahamas is also known for producing its share of celebrities, including Oscar winning actor Sidney Poitier, who was raised in the Bahamas and rock star Lenny Kravitz, whose mother was the Bahamian actress Roxie Rocker.

Most Bahamians live in the capital Nassau, and are descendants of African slaves brought to the island to work on plantations. Many can also link their ancestry to an eclectic mix of English colonists, loyalists who fled the American Revolution, and Southerners who migrated during the American civil war.

The first settlers were Arawak Indians who inhabited the islands at the turn of the 9th century. It was not until 1492 when Spanish explorer Christopher Columbus landed on Bahamian soil that the Ararwaks first encountered Europeans.

Because of its many islets and cays, the Bahamas soon became a haven for pirates and Buccaneers who used its complex shoals and channels to launch their attacks on treasure laden Spanish ships and cargo vessels. The Bahamas was an ideal place for them to attack, quickly retreat and hide their loot.

Despite the early Spanish conquest, it was the English colonists and the Africans who had the greatest influence on Bahamian culture and folklore. A number of Bahamian proverbs can be traced to the Zulus of Africa. The sea also looms large in Bahamian folklore colouring many sayings.

The people of the Bahamas speak English as well as a dialect and magically some Caribbean Indian words have survived the many centuries. For example, the names 'cassava' (a potato-like starch) and 'guava', (a sweet fleshy fruit) popular in the Bahamas and throughout the region, are thought to be of Caribbean Indian origin.

A journey through a collection of Bahamian proverbs is one way to experience some of the most profound aspects of the islands' folklore.

Bahamian Proverbs

Human Relations

When you rich don swonger and when
you poor don' cry.
*When you're rich don't brag and when
you're poor don't whine.*
It's a bad idea to boast when you're rich and
to complain when your are poor.

You shake man han', you no shake him heart.
You shake a man's hand, you don't shake his heart.
Beware of strangers.

Consequences

Seven year no 'nough for wash
speckle off guinea hen back.
*Seven years isn't enough to wash
speckles off of a guinea hen's back.*
It's difficult to change a person's nature.

Work

Hungry fowl wake soon.
A hungry fowl wakes early.
A man who needs work is anxious to find it.

Man can't whistle and smoke one time.
A man can't whistle and smoke at the same time.
It is unwise to try to do several things at once.

Sleep hab no Massa.
Sleep has no master.
Sleep is essential and cannot be avoided.

Human Nature

Misfortune nebber t'row cloud.
Misfortune never throw's a cloud.
Misfortune never stops a determined person.

Lizard no plant corn but him hab plenty.
Lizards don't plant corn but they have plenty.
There are always those who live off the avails of others.

Fish man never call e own fish stink.
The fisherman never calls his own fish stink.
People rarely acknowledge their own shortcomings or those of their family members.

Shoe know if stockin 'hab hole.
A shoe knows if a stocking has a hole.
The wise know when others are untrustworthy.

Making Choices

Follow fashion break monkey neck.
Following fashion breaks the monkey's neck.
Beware of spending to keep up with others. This behaviour can lead to bankruptcy.

Cockroach don' ask fowl to dance.
A cockroach never asks a fowl to dance.
It is unwise to put yourself in a position where your enemy can harm you.

No t'row wey dirty water befo' you hab clean.
Don't throw away dirty water before you have clean water.
It is foolish to discard old possessions before acquiring new ones to replace them.

A hungry dog will eat corn.
A desperate man can't afford to be choosy.

Every shuteye ain' sleep and every goodbye ain' gone.
Those whose eyes are shut may not be sleeping and those who say goodbye may not have left.
Beware of engaging in wrongdoing because you never know who may be watching or listening.

Spider an' fly no make bargain.
A spider and a fly never make bargains.
Beware of making a deal with your enemy.

Cunning better dan strong.
Cunning is better than strength.
Cunning can get you much farther ahead than strength.

Power

Stone at bottom of sea no know sun hot.
A stone at the bottom of the sea doesn't know that the sun is hot.
The rich often don't understand the difficulties of the poor.

Big blanket make man sleep late.
A big blanket will make a man sleep late.
Too much wealth can lead to laziness.

The higher the monkey climb, the more his tail expose.
The higher the monkey climbs, the more his tail is exposed.
The more a person climbs in social rank the more visible their flaws become.

When han' full him hab plenty company.
When a man's hand is full he has a lot of company.
People flock to those with wealth.

Hope

Time longer dan rope.
Time is longer than rope.
Time heals all wounds.

Rain nebber fall at one man' door.
Rain never falls at one man's door.
Everyone has to cope with misfortune at one time or another.

Antigua

Imagine an island where you could chose a different beach on which to frolic every day of the year. You might say that's impossible especially when the island is a mere 14 miles long and 11 miles wide. But if you venture unto the English-speaking Leeward Islands' largest and most famous island Antigua, that's what you'll find, 365 beaches with powder-like white and pink sands, spectacular coral reefs and many places to hide away, sun yourself and relax in warm, inviting Caribbean waters.

Antigua provides a window to the Caribbean Sea as well as the Atlantic Ocean and many flock to the island each year as a launching point for a sail through the numerous islands scattered across the Eastern Caribbean. Antigua is considered a haven for scuba divers and surfers. History buffs also find great pleasure exploring its historic sites, which include 18th century sugar cane plantations and old, stone cane-processing windmills, which now serve as picturesque houses, bars and restaurants.

Antigua's history tells the story of early Caribbean Indian settlements and later colonization by the Spanish, the French and the British. The Siboney or "stone people" were the first to inhabit the island. The pastoral Arawaks next found their way to Antigua, but were later driven off the island by Caribs, warriors who at various points in history dominated several Caribbean islands.

The Spaniard Christopher Columbus was the first European to set foot on Antigua and gave the country its name. But it was the British who later won the war against the fierce Caribs, colonizing the island for some 300 years. In

1834 slavery was abolished and in 1981 Antigua gained its independence.

Antigua is not only a place of intriguing history, architecture and culture, this tiny island is also the birthplace of well known author Jamaica Kincaid, whose many articles and books, including the popular *A Small Place, Lucy and Mr. Potter,* have delighted and continue to charm readers throughout the United States and the world.

Antiguans are English speaking but also express themselves through their own melodic dialect. Predominantly of African descent, they still hold on to many words and phrases that can be traced to their African ancestors. The English influence on sayings and proverbs however, is strong. The following proverbs tell the tale.

Antiguan Proverbs

Human Relations

If K ming K, he wouldn't ben' up.
If K cared for K then he wouldn't be bent up.
If people cared for each other there
would be fewer mishaps and tragedies.

Consequences

What eye no see, heart no grieve.
What your eye doesn't see, your heart won't grieve.
What you don't see won't hurt you.

Pickney no hear what mumma say, pickney
will drink water, lime and salt.
If a child doesn't listen to its mother,
it will drink water, lime and salt.
A disobedient child will suffer.

Willful waste makes woeful want.
Deliberate waste makes woeful want.
A wasteful person will eventually want.

Work

No hang yu katacoo (fish basket)
where you can' reach it.
Don't hang your hat where you can't reach it.
It is unwise to take on tasks that you
don't have the skills to complete.

A walking fool is better than a sitting fool.
An active person of limited intelligence is better than an inactive one.

A rolling stone gathers no moss.
Individuals who don't put down roots are unlikely to accumulate riches.

Human Nature

Plantain sucker follow de root.
Plantain suckers follow the root.
Like father like son.

When one monkey bray, all the rest bray wid him.
When one monkey brays, all the rest bray with him.
Monkey see, monkey do. People follow what others do.

Making Choices

A still tongue keeps a wise head.
If you speak less you are likely to learn more.

No push yu head where you body can' pass.
Don't push your head where your body can't pass.
Don't start something you can't finish.

No trust no shadow for every shadow is a man.
Don't trust a shadow, because every shadow is a man.
Be careful whom you trust because what you see may not be a man's true nature.

Joke a joke, pork a pork, but dumplin and pork make a man choke.
A joke is a joke, pork is pork, but dumpling and pork together can make a man choke.
Treating a serious matter like a joke may cause you harm.

Shut mouth no catch fly.
A shut mouth won't catch a fly.
One cannot be blamed for what one didn't say.

Ebry mouldy biscuit hab e cheese as
every monkey hab an idol.
Every mouldy biscuit has its cheese as
every monkey has an idol.
There is someone for everyone.

What hat eye mek nose run water.
What hurts the eye will make the nose run water.
If you hurt one family member you are likely to feel the wrath of other family members.

Power

Jumbie know who fe frighten before day.
A ghost knows who to frighten before daylight breaks.
People know who are weak and easily used.

Stone under water don't feel the heat of day.
A stone under the water doesn't feel the day's heat.
The wealthy have little understanding of
the trials of the poor.

Barbados

Barbados, an island known for its excellent beaches and warm climate, is also a country with unique geological features. The product of two landmasses that merged thousands of years ago, Barbados boasts caves and underground lakes that fascinate visitors and scientists alike. The most intriguing is Harrison's Cave with its amazing stalactites and stalagmites, breathtaking underground waterfalls and deep emerald pools.

Its many beaches offer miles of powdery white sand, spectacular blue-green waters and coral reefs that delight even the most seasoned scuba diver. Constant breezes from the trade winds caress the island, giving it a very agreeable tropical climate.

Like much of the Caribbean, Barbados has an Amerindian and colonial history. The Arawak Indians were the first to inhabit the island, but were later killed off by the more aggressive Caribs. When the Spanish arrived in 1492, enslavement and European diseases eventually wiped out the Caribs. Barbados however was not favoured by the Spanish and was left open for conquest by rival European countries.

In 1625 Britain claimed Barbados establishing a lucrative, sugar cane, tobacco and cotton based colonial economy. With increasing demand for sugar in Europe, the British increased production on the island, first relying on white indentured servants, criminals and even white slavery for labour.

With the advent of the African slave trade, hundreds of thousands of Africans were brought to the island as slaves to work on the sugar plantations. Slavery was abolished in 1834, however it took more than a hundred years for Barbados to eventually gain its independence in 1966.

The people of Barbados are predominantly of African descent but like much of the rest of the Caribbean, many are mixed descendants of slaves, white plantation owners, indentured servants from Britain and Asia.

The colonial history of Barbados is still very visible on the island. Old plantation mansions like St.Nicholas Abbey remain with 17th century features like curved Dutch gables, chimneystacks and coral stone finials, Chinese Chippendale staircases and fine antiques and china.

Even the baobab tree (Adansonia digitata) brought to Barbados around 1738 from Guinea in Africa still stands. Also known as the "Monkey-bread tree", it is considered possibly one of the widest tree-trunks found in the Caribbean. It actually takes 15 adults joining with outstretched arms to cover its circumference.

Land and sea aside, Barbados has produced some remarkable writers and artists, including George Lamming, John, Frank Collymore, Austin Clarke and Cecil Foster. Painters John Walcott and William Kellman are celebrated at home and abroad and of course for cricket fans, few have achieved the stature of the Bajan cricketer, Sir Garfield Sobers.

Rich with culture, history and fascinating geology, Barbados has also contributed to the reservoir of profound Caribbean proverbs. Turn the page and experience a sample of Bajan proverbial wisdom.

Bajan Proverbs

Human Relations

Home drum beat first.
Home drums beat first.
First look after your family interest, before taking on someone else's problems.

Better fish in de sea dan wha' ketch.
Better fish is in the sea than what you catch.
There is always someone that will make a better mate than the current one.

Don' leh nuhbody rub dirt in yuh mout and tell yuh it is pudding.
Don't let anyone rub dirt in your mouth and tell you it's pudding.
Don't let anyone do or say anything harmful or insulting, under the guise they are being nice.

Yuh should sell yuh butter wih yuh get yuh lard.
You should sell your butter where you get your lard.
Help those who help you.

If yuh can' beat a man yuh got tuh 'gree wid 'e.
If you can't beat a man then you should agree with him.
If you can't beat them, join them.

Rat mout does sell 'e head.
A rat's mouth will sell his head.
A loose tongue can be dangerous.

It does tek one hand tuh feel a lice, but two tuh tek it out.
It takes one hand to feel a lice and two to take it out.
Co-operation is essential if anything worthwhile is to be achieved.

Respect due to a dog.
Respect is due to a dog.
Respect is due to everyone regardless of
their social standing.

Never eat an' forget.
Never eat and forget.
Never forget the hand that fed you.

Consequences

Play wid puppy an' 'e lick yuh mout.
Play with a puppy and it will lick your mouth.
To be overly familiar with people with no scruples.
creates an atmosphere for them to treat you
with little respect.

Bucket gine up and down in well evah day,
de bottom boun' tuh drop out.
If a bucket is taken to the well every day,
the bottom will drop out.
Sustained pressure and exertion will eventually
lead to a breakdown.

Night does run 'til day ketch up wid it.
Night continues until day breaks.
Sooner or later retribution catches up
with wrong doers.

De devil does find work fuh idle hands to do.
The devil finds work for idle hands.
People with nothing to do, get themselves into mischief.

Hurry-hurry nevah dun.
Hurry, hurry never ends.
Anything done in a hurry is never done properly.

Wha' sweeten goat mout does bun 'e tail.
What is sweet to a goat's mouth can burn his tail.
A source of great pleasure may turn out to be a problem later on.

When yuh keep company wid fowls and
dey shit pon yuh table, it is hell to get out de stain.
When you keep company with fowls and
they shit on your table, it is hell to get out the stain.
Associating with undesirable people can
bring you trouble which could prove difficult to overcome.

Eat soldier food, tek soldier blows.
If you eat a soldier's food, be prepared
to take a soldier's blows.
Do not expect to share in benefits only, but
be prepared to share problems as well.

Hungry mek cat eat salt.
A hungry cat will eat salt.
Necessity often causes people to act contrary
to their regular way of life.

Yuh can' put mangoose tuh watch chicken.
You can't put a mongoose to watch chickens.
Never trust people with things, which will
be a great temptation to them.

If blackbird fly wid pigeon 'e will get shoot.
If a black bird flies with pigeons he will get shot.
Keeping the wrong company will result
in your being measured with the same yardstick.

Evah pig got a Saturday.
Every pig has his Saturday.
Everyone will pay for his deeds at some point.

When a bird fly too fast, 'e does fly past 'e nest.
When a bird flies too fast, he is likely to fly past his own nest.
Being over ambitious has its drawbacks.

When yuh pick corn pon more dan one row, yuh don' know wih yuh get yuh bag full up.
When you pick corn on more than one row you won't know where you filled up your bag.
If a woman has relations with several men, she will not be sure which one made her pregnant.

One-one blow does kill ole cow.
One blow at a time will eventually kill a cow.
What may seem like a trivial irritation may create a catastrophe if repeated often enough.

Crave all, get none at all.
Crave all and get nothing at all.
Covet everything and you may end up with nothing.

Work

Evah fool got 'e sense.
Every fool has some sense.
Everybody is knowledgeable in one area or the other, no matter how dull and ignorant they may appear.

It don't tek a big axe tuh cut down a big tree.
It doesn't take a big axe to cut down a large tree.
Size, or the lack of it, does not limit capabilities.

Good looks can' kaah tuh de shop.
Good looks can't carry you to the shop.
Physical beauty won't necessarily make you successful or marketable.

Don' rush de brush and trow 'way de paint.
Don't rush the brush and throw away the paint.
Don't let haste create problems for you.
(Haste makes waste)

Two poor cow does mek good dung.
Two poor cows make good dung.
A couple can overcome their poverty by
pooling their resources together.

Head en' mek fuh hat only.
Your head isn't made only for wearing hats
You should always use your common sense.

Ef yuh wuking wid paint you got tuh get daub.
If you're working with paint, you will get dirty.
If you are working in a particular situation,
at some point you will become affected.

Human Nature

De dog dat bring a bone will kaah one.
The dog that brings a bone will also carry one.
The person who gossips with you about other
people will also gossip with them about you.

Who help yuh buy a big guts mule don' help yuh feed it.
Who helps you to buy a big bellied mule,
doesn't help you to feed it.
The person who leads you into trouble is never around to help you get back out.

Donkey got long ear, but 'e don' like to hear 'e own story.
Donkey has long ears but he doesn't
like to listen to his own story.
People do not like to hear or accept their own faults.

Wha' hurt turkey don' hurt duck.
What hurts a turkey doesn't hurt a duck.
What may pose a problem for one person
may not have that effect on another.

Evah skin-teet en' a laugh.
Not every grin is a smile.
Not all outward signs of friendliness should
be taken as genuine.

De tongue dat buy yuh does sell yuh.
The tounge that buys you will sell you.
The one who flatters you now, may deceive you later.

Loose goat don't know wha' tie goat sih.
Loose goat doesn't know what a tied goat sees.
One has to be in someone else's shoes in order
to understand what he is going through.

Wha' evah in de ole goat in de kiddie.
Whatever is in the old goat is in the kid.
De berry don' fall far from de tree.
The berry doesn't fall far from the tree.
Children inherit the traits of their parents.

Making Choices

Fowl cock en' got nuh right in bulldog fight.
A male fowl has no right to be in a bulldog's fight.
Avoid situations that are difficult to cope with,
or those that do not concern you.

Hold de light fuh de devil tuh sih, and when yuh get a
chance, blow it out in 'e face.
*Hold the light for the devil to see and when you get a
chance, blow it out in his face*

When you know someone has bad intentions
but pretends they mean you well, play along
until the opportunity arises to foil their plans.

Yuh can' want it in de glass and de bottle too.
You can't want it in the glass and in the bottle also.
You can't have it both ways.

Mek sure better than cock-sure.
Making sure is better than being cock-sure.
It is better to make sure that everything
is all right rather than assume that all is well.

Don' wait till de horse get out de stable to shut de door.
*Don't wait until the horse leaves the
stable to shut the door.*
Don't wait until the situation gets out of control before
taking corrective action.

If greedy wait, hot wud cool.
If the anxious wait, hot will eventually turn to cool
Patience will be rewarded.

Yuh got tuh christen yuh own child before
yuh can len' out de christening clothes.
*You should Christen your own child before
lending out your child's christening clothes.*
You must solve your own problems before
trying to solve someone else's.

Don' ship all yuh sugar in one vessel.
Don't ship all your sugar in one vessel.
Do not risk all your resources in a single venture.

Never wuk ground fuh monkey run pon.
Never work the ground for a monkey to run over.
Don't exert much energy on a venture when
you know some unworthy person will benefit.

Only a dog does return to 'e vomit.
Only a dog returns to his vomit.
Once free of an offensive situation, avoid returning to it.

Evah bush is a man.
Every bush is a man.
Be careful how you talk, as you never know
who may be listening.

Power

Two smart rat can' live in de same hole.
Two smart rats can't live in the same hole.
Two tricksters can't get along with each other.

Lime juice can' spoil vinegar.
Lime juice can't spoil vinegar.
An individual can't be corrupted by another
who is less corrupt.

High wind know wih ole house live.
High wind knows where to find an old house
Duppy know who tuh frighten.
A ghost knows who it can frighten.
Advantage is often taken of those known to be weak.

Turks and Caicos

For those fortunate enough to visit the Turks and Caicos Islands, paradise is often the word that rolls off their lips. Comprised of 40 different islands and surrounded by 1,000 square miles of reef, the Turks and Caicos Islands are a world unto themselves, seemingly devoid of the noise and the bustle, that is the mark of urban living in so many other parts of our globe.

Its spectacular beauty and reputation for private alcoves have made it a haven for European royalty and many of the world's rich and famous.

The Turks and Caicos Islands have also long been regarded as a haven for scuba divers. Spectacular coral reefs line the edges of the islands, along with some of the most impressive walls of coral to be found anywhere in the Caribbean.

The deep off shore waters serve as major transit points for Humpback Whales, Manta Rays, spotted Eagle rays and Turtles.

Dolphins can be seen frolicking daily in the clear emerald green waters. Anglers also flock to the Turks and Caicos Islands in search of the rich supply of Tuna, Wahoo and Blue Marlin that inhabit the sea.

Whether your first stop is the main tourist centre of Providenciales, the tranquil islands of North and Middle Caicos, or the historic Capital Island of Grand Turk; each have a unique character and offer experiences to delight you.

Apart from world-class hotels and restaurants, well-manicured golf courses and exclusive spas, the islands offer lush woodlands, the largest cave network in the Caribbean, flamingo-filled ponds and a vast range of plant and bird life.

Its architecture gives a hint of its history, which like most Caribbean islands is a colonial one, involving Spanish, French and English occupation. The Taino Indians however, were the first to inhabit the islands. The Taino were later replaced by the Lucayan Indians and by the middle of the 16th century they too disappeared, victims of imported diseases and Spanish enslavement.

In the 17th century settlers from Bermuda established themselves on Grand Turk, Salt Cay and South Caicos, using African slaves to provide British colonies in America with salt. British loyalists fleeing the American Revolution took refuge in the islands developing a short-lived trade in cotton and sisal.

In the late 1700's the Turks and Caicos Islands briefly became a part of the Bahamas. They also were annexed to Jamaica, however after Jamaica's independence they returned to British hands as a Crown Colony.

Turks and Caicos islanders are English speaking but have retained an amazing array of African, Spanish, French, American, Jamaican and Bahamian influences within their folklore. Many of their sayings are of English origin and are similar to proverbs from other Caribbean islands. They are quite succinct and fun to read.

Turks & Caicos Proverbs

Human Relations

Come see me and come stay with me
is two different things.
You don't really get to know people until you live with them.

Cats and Dogs don't have the same luck.
To each person comes different opportunities.

Strangers don't know deep water.
Be careful of strangers.

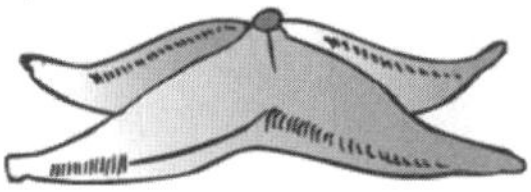

Consequences

You can't plant corn and reap potato.
You reap what you sow.

What sweeten the goat mouth burns his tail.
Not all things that are pleasurable are good for you.

You never miss the water until the well runs dry.
You never know how important something is until it's gone.

What sweet for your mouth might be bitter for your belly.
What is appealing now might give you problems later.

When you lay down with dogs, you get up with fleas.
Familiarity breeds contempt.

When you dig one pit dig two.
When you plan evil for someone it might backfire on you.

He who knows not and knows not that
he knows not is a fool.
People who don't know their limitations,
fail to realize their folly.

Work

Don't wait for the sun to go down to
know that night is coming.
Don't wait for the last minute to do things.

Leave not for tomorrow, today's work.
Never put off for tomorrow what you can do today.

Human Nature

Dog sweat but its long hair hide it.
Everyone has problems even if it's not obvious.

Sour lime doesn't fall far from the tree.
So crow the hen, so crow the chicken.
Like mother, like daughter/ like father, like son.

No fisherman say his fish stink.
People are more tolerant of their own than others.

Ain't everything that falls in the sea a shark eats.
Even the most unsavory character will
have some redeeming quality.

You can take a horse to the well but you
can't make him drink.
You can only do so much and no more.
Only the individual can decide to act.

Making Choices

If crab don't walk it don't get fat but if it walks too much, it will get put in the pot.
It is wise to use discretion in all your dealings.

Don't trust shadow after dark.
Distrust unknown circumstances.

Donkey don't run in horse race.
Always stay within your limits. Know your capabilities.

Never make your chamber larger than your hall.
Don't take things for granted.

Far off fields look green.
Beware, things often appear better than they are from afar.

You never know what's under the roof of a house.
You only know what you can see.

You walk too fast you walk two time.
Make decisions cautiously. Haste makes waste and can double your work.

Don't use a trunk when a matchbox will do.
Live within your means.

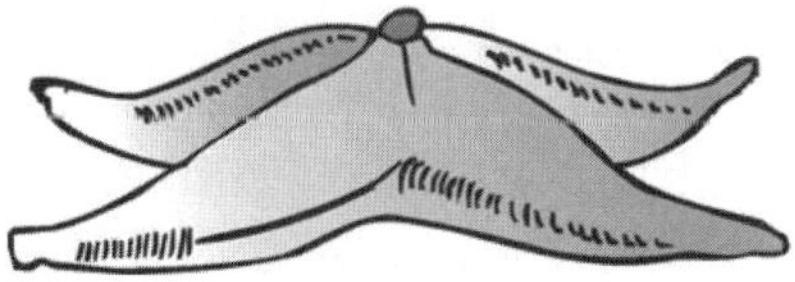

Cuba

Cuba can easily be described as one of the most controversial islands in the Caribbean. Its history is filled with battles and political intrigues that for decades have captured the imagination of historians, political scientists and everyday tourists.

The largest island in the Antilles, Cuba is long and narrow, stretching some 1,200 kilometres. Its four mountain ranges, and numerous plains, semi-deserts and tropical rainforests, make it one of the most geographically diverse islands in the region. Cuba boasts more than 300 protected areas, six of which have been declared world biosphere reserves by UNESCO.

Its moderate climate, and white sandy beaches attract thousands of tourists annually. Its music, a mix of Spanish and African influences is popular worldwide and we have the Cubans to thank for creating much loved original rhythms like the bolero, salsa, mambo and cha-cha-cha. Many music lovers appreciate this feisty island for its remarkable contributions to the evolution of Latin Jazz and of course, for lovers of a good cigar - Cuban high-grade cigars are a connoisseur's treat.

Cuba is also famous for having been the home of Ernest Hemmingway, one of the most prominent American writers of the 20th century. Recipient of the 1954 Nobel Prize for Literature Hemmingway's famous jaunts and watering holes are a huge draw for tourists. To mention only two; the restaurant El Floridita boasts a bronze statue of the American writer and T*he Old Man and the Sea*; one of Hemmingway's most famous novels is the name of a popular hotel on the island.

Cuba's history is rich and begins with the occupation of the island by the Siboney, a peaceful tribe of Caribbean Indians. Actual colonization took place in 1511 when the Spanish soldier Diego Velazquez established the town of Baracoa, some 19 years after Christopher Columbus laid claim to the island in the name of the Spanish monarchy.

However, by the middle of the 16th century mistreatment and European disease virtually wiped out the Siboney, forcing the colonists to import African slaves to work in their mines and plantations. Slavery lasted until 1886.

Throughout the 20th century, Cuba experienced a great deal of political intrigue and military activity. Its history permeates much of its folklore. While its proverbs are written and spoken in an Andalusian form of Spanish, many capture aspects of the Cuban people's African ancestry. Cuban proverbs are both provocative and profound.

Cuban Proverbs

Consequences

Camarón que se duerme se lo lleva la corriente.
A sleeping shrimp is taken by the current.
If you snooze you lose.

El que hiero mata, a hierro muere.
Who kills with iron, iron also kills.
Violence begets violence.

Al que toma y no da, el Diablo se lo llevará.
For those who take but don't give,
the Devil will take it away.
Selfish people will eventually lose
what they have selfishly gained.

Quien a buen arbol se arrima, buena sombra le cobija.
Who stands by the good tree will get the good shade.
It is best to surround yourself with good company.

Con rabia el perro, muerde a su dueño.
In anger the dog can bite his master.
Even the most loyal person will retaliate if angered.

Quien mal anda, mal acaba.
Who wrong goes, wrong ends.
Who takes the wrong path ends up in the wrong.

El que mucho abarca poco aprieta.
The one who starts many things squeezes a little.
Those who start too many things get little done.

Con la misma vara con que midas, te mediran.
*With the same stick that you measure,
you will be measured.*
If you pass judgement against others,
be prepared to be judged by the same standards.

Human Nature

Fortuna y ocasión, favorecen al osado corazón.
Luck and opportunity, favour the daring heart.
Risk takers are often lucky and attract opportunity.

Le dan un dedo, se toma la mano.
You give a finger, they take the hand.
Be careful of the greedy.
They will take all from you that they can.

A palabras necias, oídos sordos.
To stubborn words, deaf ears.
Wisdom passed on to the stubborn is never heeded.

A quien vive pobre por morir rico, llamale borrico.
Those who live to die rich, call them fools.
Those who live only to accumulate wealth are fools.

Cuando los ciegos guian, ¡ay de los que van detrás!
*When the blind are leading, look out for
those who come behind.*
The "blind" lead the "blind."

Cada uno canta como quiere.
Everyone sings as they wish.
All men and women are unique.

Making Choices

Al amigo reconciliado, con un ojo abierto y el otro cerrado.
With a reconciled friend, keep one eye open and the other closed.
Be wary of a friend who has betrayed you in the past.

Jornada emprendida, medio concluida.
A journey started is half completed.
It is wise to finish what you start.

Buenas palabras y buenos modales, todas las puertas abren.
With nice words and good manners, all doors open.
You can accomplish more with a soft touch.

No dejes camino por coger vereda.
Don't leave the road to take the path.
Be careful of the unknown.

El ojo del amo engorda al caballo.
The eye of the owner fattens the horse.
A watchful boss will reap greater benefits from his workers.

Ojos que no ven, corazón que no siente.
Eyes that don't see, heart that doesn't feel.
What you don't see won't hurt you.

A buen hambre, no hay pan duro.
For true hunger, there is no hard bread.
Stale bread is better than no bread at all.

A lo que no puede ser, paciencia.
In what cannot be, have patience.
Patience is a virtue.

No por mucho madrugar, se amanece mas temprano.
No matter how early you wake up,
it won't make dawn come earlier.
Sometimes, hurrying is useless.

Power

En el pais del ciego el tuerto es rey.
In the land of the blind, the one eyed man is king.
Those who control supply of a commodity
in demand hold power.

Caballo grande, ande o no ande.
A large horse walks or doesn't walk.
The powerful have more choices than the weak.

El que algo quiere, algo le cuesta.
He who wants something, it will cost something.
Everything costs something.

Gato con guantes, no caza, pero amenaza.
A cat with gloves doesn't hunt, but threatens.
Power is intimidating even when restrained.

Más vale ser cabeza de ratón que cola de león.
Better to be the head of the mouse
than the tail of the lion.
It is better to be a leader than a follower.

Donde se cae el burro, hay que darle los palos.
Where the donkey falls, you must beat it.
Don't let an unresolved dispute go on.

Hope

El que persevera triunfa.
He who perseveres triumphs.
Those who persevere win.

No hay mal que dura cien anos, ni cuerpo que resista.
There's no evil that lasts a hundred years,
nor a body that can stand it.
With time wounds heal.

No hay nada más verdadero que un día detrás del otro.
There is nothing more true than one day after another.
No matter how bad today is there is always a tomorrow.

El sol sale para todos.
The sun comes out for all.
There will always be bright days no matter
how many dark days surface.

Yagua que está para uno, no hay vaca que se la coma.
The heart of palm that is for you, there's no cow to eat it.
What is for you, cannot be taken from you.

El que la sigue la consigue.
He who follows her will get her.
A persistent man often wins the woman.

Agua pasada no mueve molinos.
Water that has passed does not turn the mill.
There is always a new day to try and put things right.

La esperanza es lo ultimo que se pierde.
Hope is the last thing that you lose.
With life there is hope.

References

Books

Peek, Basil. Bahamian Proverbs, Providence Press, 1966.

Beckwith, Martha Warren. Jamaica Proverbs, Poughkeepsie, 1925.

Murphy, Elaine. Antiguan Dialect.

Prahlad, Ananad. Reggae Wisdom, Proverbs in Jamaican Music by University Press of Mississippi, 2001.

Watson G Llewellyn. Jamaica Sayings With Notes on Folklore, University Press of Florida, 1991.

Caesar, Conrad. 1,000 proverbes créoles de la Caraïbe francophone.
Paris : Editions caribéennes : Agence de coopération culturelle et technique, 1987.

Magazines, Newspaper articles, Lectures

Kamau Brathwaite, History of the Voice: the Development of Nation Language in Anglophone Caribbean Poetry, 1986.

Patricia Glinton-Meicholos. Talkin' Ol Story, A Brief Survey of the Oral Tradition of the Bahamas. Lecture to the Inter-American Development Bank in Washington D.C., July 20, 2000.

Patti Hartigan, Poet Walcott of BU wins Nobel Prize, Globe and Mail, October 9, 1992.

Internet

Library of Congress Portals on the World

David P. Lichtenstein, A Brief Biography of Jamaica Kincaid, Brown University Contributing Editor, Caribbean Web, 1999

Jose M. Enguita Utrilla, Cuban Spanish Vocabulary, University of Zaragoza, Article ID 697, Cuba Heritage.com

Web sites of the Antigua and Barbuda, Cuba, Jamaica, St. Lucia, Turks and Caicos Tourist Boards and the Nobel Prize Internet Archive.

Stephen Murphy

Stephen Murphy is a self-taught artist whose talent and passion for art combine to create vibrant watercolours on canvas. Much of his work depicts scenes from Antigua, his native home, however he has also produced several paintings illustrating life in Canada. Heavily influenced by Van Gogh and the impressionist masters, Monet and Manet, Murphy has a strong attachment to brilliant colours that draw your eye to his paintings. He has lived in Canada since 1976. Samples of his work can be viewed on his web site at www.wadadli-watercolours.com

Lisa Watts

Lisa Watts is a prolific and talented graphic artist who was born and raised in Toronto Canada. Her parents are from the island of Barbados. Since graduating from York University's Visual Arts Department, Lisa has worked mainly on layout and graphic design for Afro-Caribbean publications, as well as various community newspapers in Canada. This young woman of Bajan ancestry also showcases her talents through the charcoal drawings and craft items she produces.

The Authors

Ingrid Walter is an award winning journalist and communications specialist whose work experience spans politics, television, radio and print.

Her journalistic assignments, study and travel experiences include, Canada, the United States, the Caribbean, Latin America, Europe and South East Asia. She speaks English, French and Spanish, has a Masters degree in Journalism and an honours degree in Political Science.

Originally from Jamaica, Ingrid is also known in Canada's Afro-Caribbean community for her feature articles on Canadian icons of colour and her thought-provoking opinion columns.

Sabina Theobalds has a Masters of Business Administration, with a specialization in International Business. She speaks a variety of languages including French, Spanish and Portuguese.

Her work, study and travel experience includes Brazil, Cuba, the Congo, England, France, Mexico, the United States and Wales.

In her spare time she paints and draws. Sabina, who was born in Montreal, Quebec, is of St Lucian ancestry. She lives and works in Toronto, Canada.